PICTURES · FROM · THE · PAST

London Past

PICTURES · FROM · THE · PAST

London Past

Gavin Weightman

COLLINS & BROWN

First published in Great Britain in 1991
by Collins & Brown Limited

Text Copyright © Gavin Weightman 1991

A CIP catalogue record for this book
is available from the British Library

ISBN 1 85585 057 5

The pictures in this book are archive photographs and, to preserve the character and
quality of the original, have not been re-touched in any way.

Acknowledgements
The author and publishers are grateful to the following for permission to reproduce
copyright photographs: Museum of London: 94 (Museum in Docklands Project), 96;
National Maritime Museum: 9 (far left), 88, 95.

All other photographs were supplied by the Hulton Picture Company and are available
as framed prints. For more information and to place your orders contact:

**Framed Prints
Hulton Picture Company
Unique House
21–31 Woodfield Road
London W9 2BA**

**Tel: 071 266 2660
Fax: 071 266 2414**

Conceived, edited and designed by Collins & Brown Limited,
Mercury House, 195 Knightsbridge, London SW7 1RE

Editor: Sarah Hoggett
Picture Research: Phillippa Lewis
Art Director: Roger Bristow
Designed by: Ruth Hope

Filmset by Tradespools Ltd, Frome
Reproduction by Butler & Tanner Ltd, Frome
Printed and bound in Butler & Tanner Ltd, Frome

CONTENTS

INTRODUCTION

London was *the* great world city of the nineteenth century, the first metropolis of the modern industrialised age. Though it was founded by the Romans, and was a considerable European capital in Shakespeare's day, it only became truly remarkable in the reign of Queen Victoria. A surprisingly large part of this historical period was captured in photographs. The earliest, cumbersome daguerreotypes and calotypes were developed in the 1830s and needed such a long exposure time that only static objects could be captured. But the development of photographic techniques was rapid. By the 1850s, with the use of stereoscopic cameras which took two pictures simul-

taneously, it was possible to show street scenes. When viewed in a special box the scene had the appearance of depth. This was all the rage at the Great Exhibition in London in 1851. The term 'snapshot' was coined in 1860, and in 1888 the American George Eastman was marketing the first Kodak Brownie camera.

In its heyday as a world city London was full of photographers, both professional and amateur. Of the millions of pictures that were taken probably only a fraction have survived, but even these are sufficient to conjure up a vivid vision of London Past. As historical evidence photographs can be both intriguing and frustrating. From the very first, when the pioneer Fox Talbot was experimenting with his camera, ordinary unremarkable aspects of street life would get into the picture. Later, photographers with

Scenes from a London that is almost, but not entirely lost. **FAR LEFT:** *A back yard in the dockland district of Limehouse in 1925;* **LEFT:** *Covent Garden market in the twenties – it has*

moved from its old home and is no longer a feature of street life; **CENTRE:** *street acrobats in the 1890s – forerunners of the buskers who have taken over from the fruit and vegetables*

artistic pretensions would try to compose their shots so that they had control of the contents, eliminating the mundane details of everyday life. These are often the most striking pictures from an aesthetic point of view, but not necessarily the most useful for the historian eager to recapture days gone by.

This selection of historical London photographs, drawn chiefly from the incomparable Hulton-Deutsch Picture Library, is a rich visual illustration of life in the capital from the 1870s to the 1930s. Although familiar places remain, their social use has utterly changed: the aristocratic parade in Rotten Row during the season, for example; or the Caledonian Market where poorer Londoners could buy live chickens in the twenties and thirties. Some images are frankly puzzling. Why is a flock of sheep being driven through Ludgate Circus in the 1930s?

Many others illustrate the degree to which London has lost the wonderfully rich life of the River Thames and the entire world of horse-drawn transport.

Reflected in this selection of photographs is an important historical truth about the special nature of London. In the nineteenth century, two great centres of wealth were merged and fuelled the rise of the Victorian and Edwardian suburbs. The City of London became the world's leading financial centre; and the West End, gathered around Parliament and the Royal Court, grew as the playground of the wealthy. This massive concentration of wealth drew in people seeking work and swelled the population of the capital. At the same time speculative builders and landowners began to build in a series of spectacular housing booms which covered the fields and market gardens with

in Covent Garden; **RIGHT:** *Porters from Billingsgate fish market preparing for a harvest festival: the market has now moved to a site in the West India docks;* **FAR RIGHT:** *Old*

Father Time advertising a theatrical production in Oxford Street just before the outbreak of the Great War in 1914. Sandwich board advertising was once common in London.

streets. In 1800 London's population was close to one million; by 1900 it was more than four million (or six and a half million for 'Greater London'). London continued to grow between the wars, and its physical extent *doubled* in the twenties and thirties with the building of semi-detached suburbs. Very little of London was ever planned; it grew piecemeal. It has also been continuously re-built, so that old street patterns and names remain while the buildings change. Regent Street is a good example. First carved out of the slums on the western edge of Soho in the 1820s to link the newly created Regents Park with Carlton House Terrace, most of the original stucco street designed by John Nash is gone. It was re-built, and re-opened formally in 1927, and much of the architecture shows an American influence.

Visitors to London who have been told of its 'historic' past are often puzzled as to how old bits of London are. The great mass of the metropolis is no older than parts of Washington or New York. The route of royal ceremonial along the Mall from Buckingham Palace was created in 1911 as part of a memorial to Queen Victoria. Nothing recognisable is left of the much older Mall where royalty played the game of Pell Mell and the fashionable paraded alongside St James's Park. Yet there is a sense of historical continuity in London: along the same route, the aristocracy of the 1920s and 1930s queued in their Rolls Royces with their cargoes of debutantes to be presented at the Court.

Charles Dickens said of New York: 'It gets newer every day'. The same has been true of London. But a good deal of the fascination in its

There is a century of London's history in these pictures. **FAR LEFT:** *A customer contemplating a cold winter at Caledonian Market in the thirties. You cannot buy skis or anything else there now – it has gone;* **LEFT:** *A reminder of the days when* *goods and passenger transport was horse-drawn – the drinking trough;* **CENTRE:** *The prize-giving ceremony in the thirties for the Doggett's Coat and Badge race, a competition for Thames watermen, once London's taxi*

history lies in discovering not only how much it has changed but how social continuity has been obscured by the re-working of the city's physical fabric. For example, the early underground railway lines – the Central Line (1900) and the first sections of the Piccadilly, Northern and Bakerloo lines (1907) – followed the busiest of the old horse bus routes. The promoters of the tubes, notably the flamboyant American Charles Tyson Yerkes, were businessmen and after profits. London transport remained a commercial undertaking until 1933, and its haphazard development is absolutely characteristic of a metropolis which was shaped, as it grew, by the commercial forces of the day.

If you compare London today with the impression given of the capital in this collection of photographs there is an extraordinary sensation, at one and the same time, of familiarity and of a world totally lost. Park Lane, Regent Street, St Pauls from Fleet Street, Parliament, the City streets are instantly recognisable, but they are filled with details of clothing, vehicles, shop fronts and so on that have vanished. It is as if the bone structure of the metropolis has had a remarkable durability while the fabric of life which fleshes it out has continuously changed beyond recognition.

There is a great deal to see in this collection of photographs. The section headings give a little bit of history and a context for them; the captions, wherever possible, explain them. But the more you peruse them, the more you see; and the more the photograph, as an historical document, excites an interest in London Past.

drivers. Remarkably, the race started by an actor Thomas Doggett early in the eighteenth century is still rowed today; **RIGHT:** *A Thames spritsail barge lowers its mast to go under London Bridge in the 1880s. These were the lorries of London's river, and some were still carrying cargo in the 1970s;* **FAR RIGHT:** *An ice-cream seller at St Clements Dane's in 1912 around the time this new delicacy was first introduced to the streets of the capital.*

LONDON PEOPLE

A great city is characterised not by its upper crust but by its working people, their lore and language. While it was the riches of trade in the City, and the expenditure of the rich in the West End which sustained London's population, the mass of the population was – and is – working-class.

The archetypical Londoner is the cockney, a term dating back to at least the sixteenth century. It is probably derived from the uncomplimentary term 'a cock's egg', meaning something odd and misformed; and the old definition – someone born within the sound of Bow Bell – meant someone born in the City of London itself. The term cockney was adopted with pride by Londoners.

In Victorian and Edwardian London, employers preferred to recruit servants, policemen and other staff from country districts. The cockney was a bit too sharp, a bit too streetwise, and traditionally monopolised trades in markets, cab-driving and dealing in the city. However, cockney culture has absorbed many waves of immigrants from Ireland and from Europe. For centuries, London has been at one and the same time a cosmopolitan city, unchallenged by any other in Britain as the centre of national life, and fiercely parochial in its local life.

RIGHT: *A fine turn-out of Pearly Kings and Queens for a harvest festival down the Old Kent Road in 1936. In the nineteenth century, dressing-up to collect money for hospitals was a tradition of costermongers – sellers of fruit and vegetables. The pearl-strewn outfits were the brainchild of a road sweeper in 1885: the idea caught on with the costermongers, and Pearly Kings and Queens were elected in every London borough. Attendance at a harvest festival, as here, does not imply devoutness: the cockney has not been a churchgoer by tradition.*

RIGHT: *It was the royal Court which always drew the aristocracy to the West End of London. Here guests gather for a Buckingham Palace garden party in 1935. There are now three or four such events each year, though greatly 'democratised' in their guest lists, with about 8000 people attending each event. You cannot apply to go to a garden party: you have to be invited.*

ABOVE: *A reminder of the days when even the most fashionable and wealthy of Londoners travelled by public transport – Waterloo Station, in 1934, where the fashionable still gathered to take the train to Ascot.*

LEFT: *A scallywags' fishing party to St James's Park in 1914. There were hundreds of thousands more children in London before the Great War than there were in 1939 because of the relatively high birth rate of Victorian times.*

LEFT: *Shepherdess Mrs Lily Mortimer, with her dogs Tweedie and Ben tending her flock on Hampstead Heath. Sheep grazed the Heath until the 1950s.*

BELOW: *The lake in St James's Park. Something of the spirit of the old Frost Fairs on the Thames (the last of which was held in 1814) returned to London with the severe winter of 1895.*

ABOVE AND RIGHT: *Like something out of Alice in Wonderland, the British nobility appear in their ceremonial garb outside Westminster Abbey after the coronation of George V in 1911. The manufacture of this finery, as well as that for the balls and other occasions during the aristocratic Season in London, provided work for thousands of seamstresses.*

ABOVE: *London flower girls (not all of them in the first bloom of youth) were a colourful feature of London until the Edwardian period.*

BELOW: *Ladies laden with oranges. There were many itinerant street sellers who would walk miles to sell their wares.*

Hyde Park was the playground for the offspring of the upper crust in Mayfair and Belgravia.

ABOVE: *A boy and girl, immaculately dressed, with their boat on the Serpentine in 1912.*

BELOW: *An Edwardian nanny guarding her valuable charges. In those days, London 'north of the Park' was considered almost another country, quite beyond the bounds of polite society.*

ABOVE: *A wonderful study by the great photographer of turn-of-the-century London, Paul Martin. Children tussle around an ice-cream vendor at Hampstead, a popular resort on public holidays.*

BELOW: *A bizarre game of crazy golf staged on a debris-ridden bomb site by children of the London slums – a far cry from the restrained, 'genteel' behaviour of the children on the opposite page.*

ABOVE: *A veteran of the Boer War becoming a Chelsea pensioner. The Royal Chelsea Hospital dates from the seventeenth century, and the uniforms from the eighteenth.*

ABOVE: *The giving of Maundy money by the monarch to a handful of the deserving poor. The present custom is for Her Majesty to give gifts of specially minted Maundy money to a total number of people equivalent to her age.*

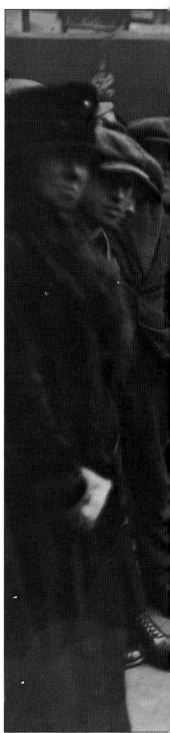

UNEMPLOYED DISABLED
EX OFFICERS
MATABELE. SOUTH AFRICA
& GREAT WAR
Both with Families to Support

ABOVE: *Wounded ex-soldiers begging. These are veterans of both the Boer War and the Great War. A few years earlier, London streets were full of crowds cheering on the soldiers who had volunteered to fight in the trenches.*

Heart of the Empire

Until the last war, London was not only the capital city of one of the most powerful nations on earth, it was the heart of an Empire on which 'the sun never set'. Its celebrations, ceremonial and entertainments took place on a national and international stage. It retains some of that atmosphere at great state occasions such as royal weddings and coronations, and with the staging of the Football Association Cup Final at Wembley which has a massive world audience. London's pageantry and its theatre remain a great attraction for the millions of tourists and its surviving aristocracy still holds a fascination abroad.

Perhaps the most remarkable aspect of the capital's changing position in the world is that it retains its magnetism even twenty years after the relinquishing of the Empire. Within the life of the nation, London remains unrivalled as the cultural and political capital.

RIGHT: *A London street party, one of many held in the capital as a popular celebration of the signing of the Peace Treaty at the end of June 1919. The terrible losses in the trenches and the national trauma of the Great War had not diminished enthusiasm for the Empire, though the hardships of the Depression and another world war were soon to follow.*

LEFT: *A celebration of the end of the Boer War in South Africa. In 1902, at the height of jingoistic fervour, the streets around Mansion House in the City were packed with revellers. By 1914, many would be volunteering to fight Germany – with Boers as their allies.*

ABOVE: *November 1918, and Londoners commandeer an early motorbus for their victory celebrations. First introduced in 1910, many of these London buses were taken to France to transport troops. Though the horrors of the trenches had been a nightmare, they were near enough to London for officers to leave France in the morning by train, and dine at a London club in the evening.*

Royal Ceremonial

A classic London scene. Crowds have waited all night to catch a glimpse of the Duke of York and his bride at their wedding in Westminster Abbey in April 1923. There was no expectation then that they would become King and Queen. After the abdication of Edward VIII, the Duke became George VI. It was not only royal weddings which drew the crowds in the twenties and thirties; aristocratic marriages were followed as the romances of film stars and pop singers are today.

BELOW: *The bridal coach.*

ABOVE AND BELOW: *Despite the appalling weather, crowds waited eagerly for a glimpse of the royal couple.*

LEFT: *A spectacular, rather old-fashioned looking shot, played by a competitor in the ladies doubles at Wimbledon in 1925. One of the great London social and sporting institutions, the All England Lawn Tennis and Croquet Club (as it is properly called) has been at its present grounds in Church Road Wimbledon since 1922. This balletic backhand is proof that back in the good old days of amateur tennis they could be serious.*

ABOVE: *Cycling was immensely popular in the 1930s. This is the finish of a rally and gymkhana at Alexandra Palace (nicknamed Ally Pally) in 1934 with more than 1,000 participants. A great increase in road traffic has made cycling much less enjoyable in the capital; but it remains, for the brave, a quick way to get to work.*

The London Season

One of the great social occasions in the calendar of the London Season was the presentation at Buckingham Palace of the débutantes 'coming out' that year – that is, officially pronounced available for marriage. The Mall was lined with limousines as the girls queued with their mothers for the Court occasion. The presentation ceremony was ended by Her Majesty the Queen in 1958, and more time given to royal garden parties to which people from a much wider social spectrum are invited. There are now three or four garden parties a year at Buckingham Palace, to which débutantes might be invited.

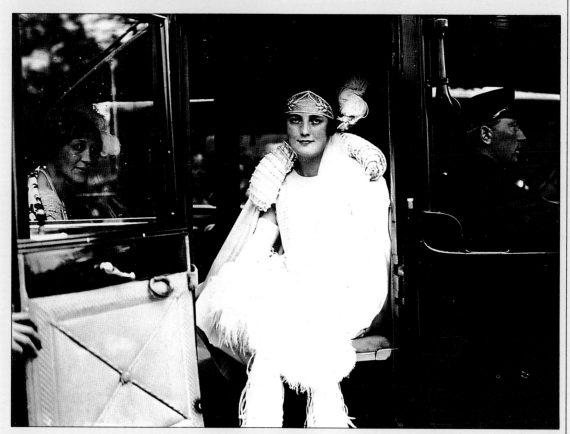

LEFT: *The dance band and the ballroom provided popular entertainment in the 1930s for a wide section of Londoners, when crazes for such numbers as The Lambeth Walk and the Chestnut Tree swept the country. Radio helped to make new numbers popular, and the dance bands would arrange favourites to their own particular style. This is Roy Fox and his band at the Monseigneur Grill.*

ABOVE: *First nights of London plays have always attracted the glitterati. This distinguished guest is about to be amused by Noel Coward's* Private Lives *at the Phoenix Theatre in 1930. Laurence Olivier was in the cast. It was the first night not only for the play, but also for the Phoenix Theatre itself, built in Charing Cross Road on the site of an old music hall, the Alcazar.*

Hampstead Heath

All the fun of the fair on Hampstead Heath during the August Bank holiday in the 1920s. This wonderful open tract of land, covering 800 acres, has since late Victorian times been one of the favourite resorts of Londoners. It was very nearly built over in the mid-nineteenth century when the owner of the land, Sir Maryon Wilson, applied for an Act of Parliament to create yet another suburb here. But fortunately for countless generations of Londoners he lost a fierce battle both in the courts, in Parliament and on the ground; and in 1871 the Heath was saved. Annual fairs are still held there. Until recently the Heath was in the charge of the Greater London Council, but since the abolition of the capital's metropolitan authority in April 1986 it is not clear who will care for it in the future.

ABOVE: *Stoke City supporters, arriving in London to watch their team play Arsenal in March 1928.*

LEFT: *Soccer fans of the Edwardian era in London for the 1906 Cup Final in which Everton beat Newcastle United by one goal to nil. Modern football or soccer began as a public schoolboys' game, and the first Cup Finals, which started in 1871, were between schools. But it became popular in industrial areas, and after the Old Etonians were beaten by Blackburn Olympics in 1883 it became a predominantly working-class game.*

ABOVE: *Theatre crowds during the Great War. It was mostly vaudeville which had to compete with the silent cinema for a popular following. With the exception of musicals and pantomime, the theatre became more exclusive between the wars.*

LEFT: *A huge crowd at the Canterbury Music Hall in Westminster Bridge Road, Lambeth. In the heyday of this form of entertainment in the 1880s and 1890s, there were 68 music halls in London providing cheap, popular entertainment. In his unhappy childhood, the great cinema comedian Charlie Chaplin saw his father perform at the Canterbury.*

RIGHT: *One of the first 'Talkie' cinemas in 1929. The heyday of films came when the sound was synchronised with the picture, from the time of Al Jolson in* The Jazz Singer *in 1927. By the 1930s, cinema had killed off the music hall and provided unheard-of cheap luxury for the masses. In some areas, half the population went to the cinema once a week.*

London Pubs

Much to the horror of the Victorian reformers and the Temperance Movement, the London public house, which had its heyday of building in the 1880s, has long been the most popular resort for the mass of the population. The imposition of 'closing hours' during the Great War greatly reduced drinking though recently the law has once again been relaxed.

TOP: *Ye Olde Cheshire Cheese in Fleet Street was a 'chop house' famous for its huge puddings containing oysters and larks.*
BOTTOM: *Charlie Brown's, which was famous for its exotic collection of trophies brought from all over the world by sailors.*
RIGHT: *The White Horse public house and Half Moon hotel.*

SHOPPING

For hundreds of years London has been by far and away the biggest market in the country for all kinds of goods. Its shopping style in the West End was transformed in the late Victorian period by the rise of department stores, such as Harrods in Knightsbridge or Barkers and Derry & Toms in Kensington. These grew from relatively small shops to serve the growing Victorian middle class. Whereas the aristocracy had traditionally run up large amounts of credit with shop-keepers in Mayfair or Regent Street, and their servants did much of the shopping demanding 'cook's perks' from grocers and butchers in return for the custom of their mistresses, the new stores abolished these practices.

In local high streets there were many markets and the small shop survived, often with the owner and family living above the premises. The contrast between the East End and the West End of London was very sharp. A great deal of the clothing for the richer areas was made in the East End, but the best shops were all, naturally, in the West End where their customers lived or stayed during the Season. During the nineteenth century shops had begun to disappear from the city and follow the fashion westwards. By the late nineteenth century, London was the shopping centre not only for the whole metropolis but for people from the provinces who could travel to the capital and back home again by train.

RIGHT: *Oxford Street in 1909, the year Selfridges opened. It was considered a bold and unwise move to build such a large store here to rival Harrods because Oxford Street was regarded as being on the fringes of the fashionable area. But the American Gordon H. Selfridge ignored the snobberies of London and attracted huge crowds with a new brash kind of publicity and luxury in the store. Oxford Street has been re-built in many parts since this photograph was taken, but Selfridges is still there as a great London landmark which few would regard now as American-inspired.*

ABOVE: *A classic tale of rags to riches. A. W. Gamage, a farmer's son who was apprenticed to a draper in the City in the 1870s, began his own little shop with a few pounds. This grew bit by bit into one of the great department stores of the early twentieth century, though it was in Holborn, outside the main shopping area of the West End. Pictured here in its heyday, in 1923, it sold a wonderful range of goods, including cars, and had a mail order catalogue in the Edwardian era. Sadly it closed in 1972 and all trace of it has gone.*

ABOVE: *A fine window display of the 1920s. Empire Day and Empire Week were celebrated each year, and the people of London, along with the rest of the country, were encouraged to 'buy British' in order to help the national economy which had suffered loss of trade in the Great War.*

ABOVE: *Fortunately, not all of London's shops have grown into great department stores or chains. In areas like Soho, the small shop still survives – though none is quite as diminutive as this cobbler's in Batemen Street, photographed around 1900 and claiming, evidently with some justification, to be the smallest shop in London.*

ABOVE: *A survivor from the days when there were many shops in and around the City of London, before the trend of shopping moved westwards in the later Victorian period. These two gents are solemnly celebrating fifty years as costumiers Messrs Spreckley, White and Lewis of Cannon Street.*

ABOVE: *A lady is fitted with a 'Mermaid Dress' at Fifinella's in the West End for her presentation at Court in 1923.*

RIGHT: *A house in Whitechapel, East London, becomes a makeshift clothes shop in 1938, just before the war. As these two pictures illustrate, East and West were – and still are – two quite different worlds in London.*

London Foodshops

London foodshops before the supermarket. In those days, the shopkeeper came to the customer. A great deal was delivered, and there were many more street sellers than there are today.

ABOVE: *A greengrocers in St Martins Court off Charing Cross Road in 1910.*

RIGHT: *During the Great War women took over many of the delivery jobs that had been almost exclusively men's work. They drove carts and rode bicycles.*

ABOVE: *Castor Street in London's original Chinatown which grew up around Limehouse in the dockland area. Here Chinese seaman who came over on the East India Company's tea clippers would jump ship and stay in London. The Chinese were known for their opium smoking and involvement in London's dockland underworld. Gerrard Street in the West End became the main area for Chinese restaurants and shops around the 1950s.*

ABOVE: *This area of Clerkenwell used to be known as 'Little Italy'. London's Italian community were originally artisans from the northern parts of Lombardy who came to work as instrument makers and craftsmen in the Hatton Garden area. They brought with them their own shops, like this one pictured just at the back of the Farringdon Road in 1907. Later, immigrants became ice-cream salesmen, and opened restaurants which are still mostly done out in an 'alpine' style.*

MARKETS

The feeding of London's vast and growing population required meat, fish and fruit and vegetable markets from the earliest times. The City of London, a law unto itself, had control of all markets within a seven-mile radius, including Smithfield where cattle were driven in on the hoof to be slaughtered and Leadenhall market specialising in poultry, game and hides. Though there were unlicensed markets, all the major ones needed official sanction of some kind.

There are still many street markets in London but, with the re-siting of the wholesale markets and the rise of supermarket shopping, a great deal of the colour has gone. In the days of Charles Dickens, just about everything could be bought from street sellers, including song-birds which were trapped in fields on the outskirts of London, now built over. A great deal of produce was once carried into town. Large armies of women would bring in the delicate strawberry crop in baskets balanced on their heads, walking up to twenty miles in a day.

RIGHT: *Covent Garden, the fruit, vegetable and flower market which grew up informally in the seventeenth century on the estate of the Dukes of Bedford, photographed in 1910. It was granted a charter by Charles II and, in Victorian times, expanded enormously into the largest market of its kind in London. The Piazza was originally a residential square, but became the centre of the market when it was re-developed in the 1860s by the Bedford estates which made a great deal of money from it. The market finally moved in 1973 and the area has been taken over by shops and restaurants. It narrowly escaped demolition and comprehensive re-development after a long fight by preservationists.*

Covent Garden Market

Scenes from the great fruit, vegetable and flower market in Covent Garden in the twenties and thirties, when motor lorries were beginning to replace horse-drawn carts. When these photographs were taken, many of the old skills and traditions still survived.

LEFT: *A porter practises in 1930 for the annual basket-carrying competition in the market.*
ABOVE: *Women shelling peas.*
BELOW: *A 'whip lady', who looked after the carters' whips while they delivered or collected goods.*

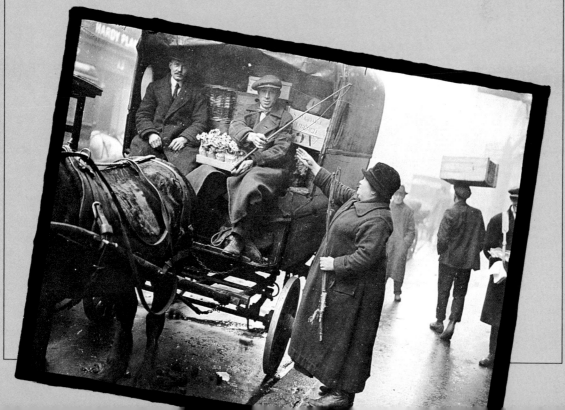

LEFT: *Club Row, where London's song-birds have been sold for centuries. Before protection of birds and the outlawing of trapping, vast numbers of goldfinches, bullfinches, linnets, thrushes and other song birds were trapped in the countryside around London and sold here or on the streets. Fanciers took great pride in the 'piping' of their bullfinch or the song of their thrush, and in the pubs would hold singing competitions between caged birds, on which there was usually gambling. Native British birds are still sold, illegally unless they have been bred from captive stock. It is thought the French Huguenot settlers brought bird-fancying to this part of East London in the eighteenth century.*

The Cally

Gone now, converted into playing fields, housing and a park, is one of North London's largest markets, known affectionately as the Cally. Originally opened to take livestock when this was banned from Smithfield in 1855, this was the Metropolitan Cattle Market. The City Corporation built the new market, with its imposing clock tower which still survives. On days when no livestock was being sold, odds and ends were traded here, and gradually this took over. It became known as Caledonian Market after the nearby Caledonian Road. You could still buy a chicken live and kicking here in the 1920s, but it was known principally for its bric-a-brac bargains. It closed in 1965.

RIGHT: *Billingsgate fish market, on the river just below London Bridge and formerly one of the gates to the walled city, pictured in the 1930s. Fish was originally brought in by boat from the river or the North Sea. (Barking in Essex had the biggest fishing fleet in Britain in the early 1800s, preserving its North Sea catch with ice cut from fields in winter and shipping it up to Billingsgate.) On the left are two porters with the flat hats used for carrying fish boxes on their heads. The market left its Victorian building in 1982 and is now in the re-developed West India docks.*

LEFT: *Just before the Great War in 1913, a toy seller hawks his wares on Ludgate Hill hoping for custom from City commuters.*

BELOW: *Sandwich-board men were taken seriously in Edwardian London. These have been rigged out to spell the name of a small manufacturer of motor cars from Leicester Square exhibiting at the third motor show at Olympia in 1908.*

RIGHT: *A London costermonger (he is the one with the silk cravat) in 1877. At one time there were around 30 000 costermongers in the capital. We have an unusually detailed description of this photograph, from the famous book* Street Life in London *by John Thompson. The costermonger is Joseph Carney and his fish stall was in a street market between Seven Dials and Five Dials on the edge of Covent Garden. The boy with the pitcher is 'Little Mic-Mac Gosling', 17 years old and only three feet ten inches tall, and he is fetching spring water to bathe a lady's foot. His own bare feet are due not so much to poverty as to a habit he acquired as a sailor.*

STREETS

One of the most fascinating aspects of London's history is the persistence of a pattern of streets and places through hundreds of years of re-development. It is very confusing for the tourist, for many buildings have gone up in some 'historic' style, along ancient roads, giving the impression that they are very much older than they are. From the time most of the City of London was destroyed by the Great Fire of 1666, grand plans for re-designing the capital have been put forward, but they have always failed. The shape of London has been determined by market forces and piecemeal re-development rather than by the schemes of the planners.

The life of the streets has changed out of all recognition since the Victorian era, so that there is a 'double take' when you see a familiar view from a century ago. It is instantly recognisable as a London vista, but inhabited in a completely different way. The biggest single factor changing the nature of streets has been the motor car.

RIGHT: *An extraordinary panorama of Whitehall around 1910, when much of the area was being re-built as government offices. There is so much going on in this one scene that it is almost like a stage set, with a horse-drawn bus crawling through a traffic jam, roadmen working, a girl with a pram, and*

ABOVE: *Regent Street in the heart of London's West End around 1910. There is a motor car among the horse-drawn carriages. Once the fashionable shopping street for the aristocracy, by this time it was attracting the middle classes from all over London. The famous Libertys, founded to sell fabrics from the East, is on the right. An entirely new store was built in the 1920s when nearly all of this part of Regent Street had been re-developed.*

ABOVE: *A classic West End street scene at the turn of the century, with bicycle and horse-drawn traffic – before the motor car came to dominate the capital.*

LUDGATE HILL & CIRCUS FROM FLEET STREET. 4523.

L.S.&.P.Co.

Continuity

Both these scenes provide illustrations of the way in which streets appear to have changed little in the intervening years while their character, and the details of everyday life which fill them, have altered almost beyond recognition.

ABOVE: *A sherbert drink seller in Cheapside in the City around the turn of the century (photograph by Paul Martin).*

LEFT: *The view down Fleet Street to Ludgate Hill and St Paul's in the 1890s. Note the steam train crossing on its way out of Farringdon Station; this bridge was recently demolished.*

RIGHT: *Livestock were once a common sight in London's streets as they were driven in to butchers and meat markets to be slaughtered. These sheep were pictured at Ludgate Circus in 1937 – possibly on their way to graze in Hyde Park.*

ABOVE: *A performing bear in a Victorian suburban street around the turn of the century. In this sort of neighbourhood few people would own their own carriage, and at that time nobody had a car – so the road is empty.*

TRANSPORT

L ondon's commuter bus services began in 1829 when George Shillibeer brought over a Parisian invention, the omnibus. His pioneer route from Paddington to the City failed because hackney cab drivers had a monopoly in the City of London. But by the 1850s a network of horse bus routes was established, run by a French company. Only the wealthy could afford the bus. Hundreds of thousands of commuters walked to work. In 1910 motor buses replaced London's horse buses, and the horse-drawn hackney cabs rapidly disappeared. But horses still hauled many goods vehicles until the Second World War. A remarkable feature of the Victorian era was the massive increase in the demand for horses brought about by the railways. The trains got people and goods from one town to another – but *within* London there was only horse-power. Until the early 1900s, hay and oats were the main source of fuel for London Transport.

The first underground railway was the Metropolitan Line opened in the 1860s with steam trains. This was not the tube proper – the tunnels were built by 'cut and cover'. The first electric underground railway ran from Stockwell to the Bank in 1890. The Central Line followed in 1900, and the other central lines in the Edwardian era. Many of the station exteriors with their ox-liver coloured tiles survive. The great form of working men's travel, the horse tram followed by the electric tram, has now completely disappeared.

RIGHT: *A classic London scene from 1924. On a rainy night, a policeman holds up the traffic, including an open-topped bus, to allow MPs to cross Parliament Street to go to the House of Commons. Buses with a roof did not appear until 1925. London transport was privately run in those days (until 1933 in fact) and was dominated by the Underground Group which controlled both buses and tube trains.*

LEFT: *A growler picking up luggage around 1920. Motor taxis had first appeared in the early 1900s, but horse-drawn growlers and hansoms survived until the 1940s. Today's motor cabs are licensed by the Metropolitan police and all drivers have to pass a test on their knowledge of London. It can take two years for a driver to learn 'The Knowledge'.*

ABOVE: *A four-wheeled or 'growler' cab with an unusual load on its roof in 1914. Hansom cabs had two wheels and no seat for a third passenger next to the driver. The numbers of both kinds of cab – an abbreviation from the French* cabriolet *– increased to such an extent in the late Victorian and Edwardian period that they were regarded as the cause of terrible jams.*

LEFT: *The changing face of Rotten Row in Hyde Park in 1921. It was here the Victorian and Edwardian aristocracy paraded on horseback in the Season. The motorbike was not entirely appropriate for this kind of socialising, and was a novelty that did not catch on.*

LEFT: *Cart-horses and a boy refresh themselves during a heat-wave in 1932. This London oasis was almost certainly provided by the Metropolitan Drinking Fountain and Cattle Trough Association, originally founded in the mid-nineteenth century to provide wholesome water in poor districts.*

ABOVE: *The first electric trams, which replaced the horse-drawn trams, ran in 1901. This is a picture of the Prince of Wales, later George V, at a ceremonial tramway opening in Westminster Bridge Road in 1903. A few years later, in 1910, the electric tram faced fierce competition from the motor bus.*

RIGHT: *No traffic lights here at the busy junction between Oxford Street and Regent Street in 1928. Note the 'Please Cross Here' sign toward the bottom right-hand corner, and the couple ignoring it in the middle of the fray. There was less traffic about then, but it was inefficiently managed: there were no driving tests until 1935.*

ABOVE: *Trolley buses, powered by electricity from overhead cables but running on rubber wheels, not rails, began to replace trams in 1935. But by the 1950s, when all the trams had gone, the trolley buses were on the way out too. Whereas other cities have kept their trams and trolley buses, London could never tolerate the inconvenience they caused to the more mobile car. In the long term, this may turn out to have been short-sighted.*

London Transport

Scenes from the heyday of London Transport in the twenties and thirties. The Underground was then admired all over the world. Those sections constructed early in the century were built largely with private money.

ABOVE: *The control room of Wood Green substation on the Piccadilly line. To relieve unemployment government money went into the Underground extensions and improvements in the inter-war years.*

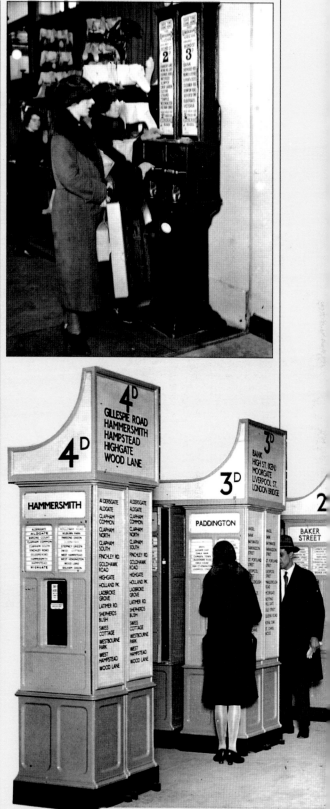

TOP RIGHT: *Vending machines for tube tickets in Selfridges store in 1923.*

BOTTOM RIGHT: *Ticket machines at Piccadilly station 1928, then the very height of modernity.*

Gateway to the West

Two evocative scenes at London's Paddington station, terminus of the Great Western Railway, opened in 1838. The demand for passenger travel in and out of London was not anticipated by the first railway promoters, but commuting on a large scale had become popular by the 1860s. Paddington station to the west of London was linked with the east and the great goal of the commuter, the City, in 1863 by the first underground railway, the Metropolitan.

ABOVE: *Unloading milk churns at Paddington during the General Strike of 1926. The milk got through; the strike failed.*

LEFT: *A graphic photograph of Paddington station early one morning in 1933.*

THE THAMES

In the past thirty years or so, the River Thames has sadly lost nearly all of its importance for London. Once the busiest river in the world, its powerful tides carrying sailing barges, tugs, cargo ships and lighters into the heart of the capital day and night, it is now almost deserted. Above Teddington Weir, the non-tidal, freshwater reaches associated with the dreamy world of Henley, the Thames remains a wonderful playground for Londoners and the people of Reading, or Oxford or Maidenhead. But what has gone, perhaps forever, is the commercial life of the river.

The historic significance of the Thames for the growth of London is easily forgotten now, in the age of air travel and the motor lorry. It was a vital highway for the capital, linking London with the industrial north-east and the rest of the world. The tides run a long way inland, so coal and grain, stone and timber could be brought right into the centre of the metropolis and unloaded in the docks and riverside warehouses. Within London, an enormous quantity of goods was shipped around on the river by lightermen. Though the largest area of enclosed dockland in the world was built to the east of the City from the early 1800s, London remained a river port to the end, with mile upon mile of riverside warehouses. Now the port is a long way east at Tilbury in Essex and an entire world has disappeared. It collapsed between 1967 and 1982 and much is now being redeveloped as housing and offices.

RIGHT: *The Pool of London, the centre of the old river port, just below London Bridge in 1945. On either bank, down to Tower Bridge and well beyond, the river is lined with warehouses. In the foreground are lighters, and two steam tugs, which took cargoes from ships and distributed them all along the Thames. Traffic on the river was cut by about three-quarters during the Second World War, but it picked up again in the 1940s and 1950s and did not disappear until the 1970s.*

RIGHT: *A wonderful illustration of the versatility of both river transport and the horse-drawn cart. In 1934, a spritsail barge has beached at Lambeth – these vessels were flat bottomed and could moor almost anywhere – and is loading sand and gravel into horse-drawn carts at low tide. A great deal of London's building material was brought in in this way.*

ABOVE: *Two canal narrow boats moored on the Thames opposite St Paul's Cathedral in 1901. In the centre of London the river was linked with the Grand Union Canal through Regent's Canal dock. Although the railways took away a great deal of canal trade in the nineteenth century, coal and other bulk goods were still carried in narrow boats from the docks. Narrow boats would also come all the way down the Thames from places like Weybridge.*

RIGHT: *Tower Bridge in 1900, just six years after it was completed as the last bridge between London and the sea. It was and remains, one of the great sights in London, its steel frame clad in stone to blend in with the Tower of London. The children in the foreground seem more interested in the water.*

RIGHT: *The old Chelsea suspension bridge around 1870. Like most of the bridges built across the Thames in central London it was financed from toll charges. The toll-gate houses are on either side. To ease the flow of traffic most of the tolls disappeared in the 1870s when the Metropolitan Board of Works bought out private interests and took the bridges into public ownership. The present Chelsea Bridge replaced this one in 1934.*

LEFT: *Old Waterloo Bridge in 1921. It had been built in 1811, but began to crumble two years after this photograph was taken. A battle over the re-building of it raged in the 1930s. The London County Council insisted on pulling it down, despite protests from Westminster, and it was replaced by the present bridge during the war.*

LEFT: *Not a normal day on London's riverside. This was the scene at Hays Wharf by London Bridge in May 1926 during the General Strike when volunteer workers came in to take over from dockers to unload perishable supplies of bacon, eggs and butter. Today Hays Wharf is re-developed as offices, shops and restaurants and all the dockers have gone.*

LEFT: *A flotilla of Thames spritsail barges on the way into a dock – probably the Surrey Docks on the south side, where most of London's timber was unloaded. These sailing barges were traditional on the Thames, some going as far as Cornwall, but most working between London and the coasts of Kent and Essex. Their ingenious design enabled them to be worked by just two men, which kept down costs and made them economic to run until the 1970s. Those that remain are all now pleasure boats of one kind or another.*

ABOVE: *A vision of London's riverside from the time when it really was a sailing port – probably the 1860s. This is Wapping where the ships in the coasting trade moored to unload their cargoes of coal brought from the north-east of England. The celebrated riverside pub, the Prospect of Whitby, was probably named after one of these collier ships.*

ABOVE: *Sunrise over the Thames in the 1930s, showing the Thames crowded with lighters between London Bridge and Tower Bridge to the east. No part of the capital has changed as much in the past half century as the riverside east of London Bridge. It is much less colourful than it was, but the river itself is much cleaner. More than 100 species of fish, including salmon, have been recorded for the central reaches of the Thames since it was cleaned up in the 1960s.*